WHERE YOU LIVE

GOING SHOPPING

Ruth Nason

Photography by Chris Fairclough

FRANKLIN WATTS
LONDON • SYDNEY

First published in 2007 by
Franklin Watts
338 Euston Road
London NW1 3BH

Franklin Watts Australia
Level 17/207 Kent Street
Sydney NSW 2000

ISBN 978 0 7496 7174 7

Dewey classification number: 381'.1

A CIP catalogue record for this book is available from the British Library.

Planning and production by Discovery Books Limited
Editor: Paul Humphrey
Designer: Ian Winton
Photography: Chris Fairclough

Printed in China

Franklin Watts is a division of Hachette Children's Books.

Photo acknowledgements
All the photographs in this book were supplied by Chris Fairclough except for the following: page 24 (top) Maurice Ambler/Picture Post/Getty Images.

Note about questions in this book
The books in the Where You Live series feature lots of questions for readers to answer. Many of these are open-ended questions to encourage discussion and many have no single answer. For this reason, no answers to questions are given in the books.

Contents

Going shopping

A shop is a building or a room where things are bought and sold.

Many shops have a front window to display their **goods**.

- What goods are for sale in the shops on these two pages?

- In the picture below, what might the shopkeeper and the customer be saying to each other?

Inside a shop, the shopkeeper or shop **assistants** serve the **customers**.

When you go shopping, you choose what you want and find out the price. You hand over the money in exchange for the item.

WHERE YOU LIVE
Look at shop window displays. Find the one that you think is best.

- Which is your favourite shop?
- Why do you like it?
- If the price is £1.50 and you give a £5 note, how much change does the shop assistant give you?

The money is put into the **till**. The shopkeeper uses the money to

- pay for the shop building
- pay the people who work in the shop
- pay the people who provide the goods to sell in the shop.

Shopping at a market

Long ago there were no shops. Most people grew their own food, kept animals and made things for themselves.

Some people grew more food than they needed. They took it to the village centre, to sell or to exchange for something else. This is how markets began.

WHERE YOU LIVE
Use the index of a local street atlas to find towns that have a 'Market Place', 'Market Square' or 'Market Street'.

- What goods are for sale at the market **stall** on the left of this picture?

- What markets are held in or near your town or village? (You could do an internet search for 'market days' and the name of your town or county.)

- On which days are the markets held?

On market days today, **traders** set up their stalls to sell all kinds of things. Many of the goods are cheaper than in shops. Some traders call out what they have to sell.

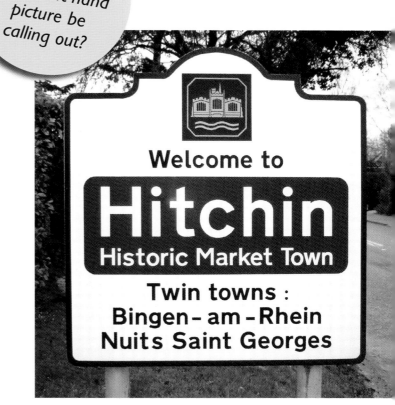

• What could the man in the left-hand picture be calling out?

Some towns are called market towns. The markets there were once the main places to buy and sell for people all around.

Market towns have a wide main street or a large square. This was where the market was held. Markets are still held in the squares of many market towns.

Small shops

The number of people in a village is quite small, and so a village shop is small. This one sells **groceries**, newspapers and **stationery**. It is also a post office, where people can send letters and parcels.

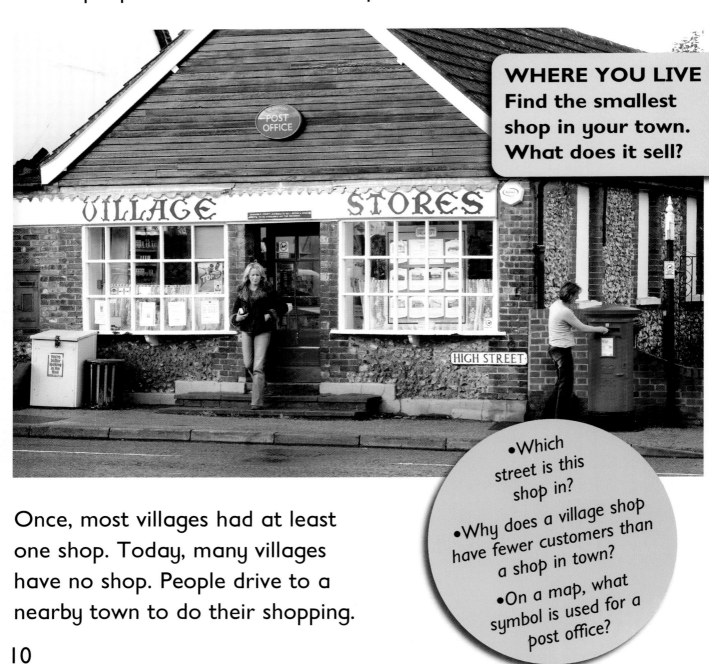

WHERE YOU LIVE
Find the smallest shop in your town. What does it sell?

Once, most villages had at least one shop. Today, many villages have no shop. People drive to a nearby town to do their shopping.

- Which street is this shop in?
- Why does a village shop have fewer customers than a shop in town?
- On a map, what symbol is used for a post office?

A shop can be small if it stocks small goods. The shop above is a part of one room. The goods are displayed on the **counter**.

In the street below, the smaller shop is a **travel agent**. People go there to look at holiday **brochures** and to book holidays.

- What is the travel agent called in the picture below? Why do you think it is called this name?
- What happens to the goods in a flower shop if people do not come to buy them?
- Which needs to be bigger: a flower shop or a furniture shop?

Big shops

A **supermarket** is big. It stocks large numbers of goods. The goods are put out on shelves so that customers can take what they want. There must be space between the shelves for customers to carry baskets or push trolleys.

- What are the names of supermarkets in your town?
- What colour are the trolleys at the supermarket where you go?
- How do you travel to the supermarket?

A supermarket has many **checkouts** where customers go to pay.

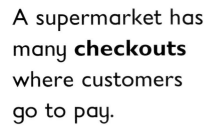

WHERE YOU LIVE
Notice all the jobs that people do in a supermarket. Make a display about it.

Another big shop is a **department store**. It has many sections with different things for sale, from shoes to beds. This is a famous department store in London.

- How many checkouts are there at the supermarket where you go?
- In a big department store, how do customers go from one floor to another?

Where are shops?

This shop is on its own, on the corner of two streets of houses. It is called a 'store' because it stocks many things that people need. 'Convenience' means being easy. The shop is convenient for the people who live in the streets round about.

FIRST STOP
OFF LICENCE
PAYZONE
NEWSPAPERS
MOBILE TOP UP

off licence

YEOVIL ROAD

FIRST STOP CONVENIENCE STORE

Premier

FIRST STOP CONVENIENCE STORE

only £9.99

any 2 for 90p

any 2 for £2

ICE CREAM
CIGARETTES
NEWSPAPERS
GREETING CARDS

- Why is this shop called 'First Stop'?
- What things can people buy at the shop?
- Why do you think the shop is painted red and yellow?
- Which is the nearest shop to your home?
- What does the shop's **logo** tell you about the things for sale in the shop?

WHERE YOU LIVE
Find the list of convenience stores in your local telephone directory. What names do the shops have?

Usually, shops are grouped together in the village or town centre.

Some large shops are grouped in a **retail park** or shopping centre near the edge of the town or city.

•In your town or city, how many shops have flats above them?

•Why do people like to park their cars near the shops?

Town centre shopping

Many people drive to the town centre to go shopping. They must find a place to park.

Traffic can drive and park in some streets of shops. But some shopping streets are closed to traffic. This makes a **shopping precinct** like the one below.

- Where can people park when they come to shop in your town or city?
- How much does it cost to park?
- What do you think is good about the shopping precinct in the bottom picture?

P Church Road (Shoppers)

WHERE YOU LIVE
Write about the shopping area of your town centre – the sights, sounds, smells and how you feel when you go there.

16

There are different names for different groups of shops.

- A row of shops along a street is a **parade**.
- An **arcade** (below) is a covered passageway, with shops on both sides.

- A shopping **mall** is a very big building that contains many shops.

- Why is the man on the left of the top picture sitting down?
- What differences are there between a mall and a street of shops?
- Do you prefer to be in a mall or in a street?

What shops are in your town?

You could do a survey of shops in your town or city centre. Sort them into groups, such as:

- grocer's shops
- **take-aways**
- clothes shops
- card and gift shops
- **newsagents**
- mobile phone shops
- carpet shops
- travel agents
- **estate agents**, where people go to buy, sell or rent houses and flats
- **charity shops**
- other shops.

Also count how many **banks** and **building societies** there are.

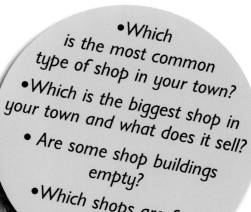

- Which is the most common type of shop in your town?
- Which is the biggest shop in your town and what does it sell?
- Are some shop buildings empty?
- Which shops are for young people?

At some shops you do not buy goods. You pay for someone to do a service for you. Shops like this include:

- barbers and hairdressers
- dry cleaners
- shoe menders
- bicycle and car repair shops.

• Which types of services are provided in shops in your town?

FREE
1st
SERVICE
WITH
ALL
NEW BIKES
WITHIN 2 MONTHS
OF PURCHASE
cycleworks.co.uk

WHERE YOU LIVE

Find out about changes. Ask grown-ups if they remember shops in the town that are no longer there. Also look for shops that are closing down and new shops that are opening. Think about why the changes happen.

Charity shops

A charity is an organisation that helps people in need, such as people who are very poor or very ill.

Many charities have shops. When people buy things from a charity shop, the money goes to the charity.

- What do you know about the charity Oxfam?
- Which charity shops are in your town or city?
- Who or what are the charities working to help?
- Do you support a charity?

People also give things for charity shops to sell. This lady is taking a bag of goods to a **hospice** charity shop.

WHERE YOU LIVE
See if you have toys that you don't want any more. Could you give them to a charity shop?

The things that people give to the shop are sorted in the **stock room** (right).

The prices are quite low, because the goods are **second-hand**.

Most charity shop workers are **volunteers**.

- What things have people given for the charity shop on this page to sell?
- Do you sometimes buy second-hand things from a jumble sale or car boot sale?

Attracting customers

Shopkeepers need customers to come to their shops and buy things. If you were a shopkeeper, what would you do to attract customers? Here are some ideas.

- Choose a good name for the shop.
- Display the name so that people notice it.

WHERE YOU LIVE
Look for clever shop names that are fun, such as 'Bed-E-Buys' for a bed shop.

- Have your shop in a street where many people go.
- Make the shop easy for people to enter and move around in.

- Why is a musical instrument shop called 'Hooters'?
- In the picture on the left, what is an 'automatic door'?
- What type of shop entrance is difficult for people with pushchairs or wheelchairs?
- In your town, what has been done to help people who have a disability?

- Make attractive displays of your goods.
- Play music in the shop.
- Have seats and a coffee bar for customers.
- Be friendly and helpful and know about the goods that customers come to buy.

- Do you know some shops where music is played? How does it make you feel?
- What does the shopkeeper on the right need to know about the goods in his shop?
- Do you have a favourite shopkeeper or shop assistant? Why do you like them?

Shopping then and now

The top photo shows a grocer's shop in the 1950s. Then, customers asked at the counter for everything they wanted. Now, most food shops and other shops are **self-service**, like the one below.

•What differences would there be between going shopping in the two shops on this page? Is it quicker to shop in a self-service shop? Is it as friendly?

In the past, shops were owned by local shopkeepers. Now, large **companies** own **chains** of hundreds of shops all over the country.

Shops today sell more types of goods than in the past. They stay open for longer in the evenings, too.

People shop at all times on the internet. The goods are delivered to their home.

●How many hours each weekday is this shop open?
●Which shops in your town are part of chain owned by a company?
●Can you find out why some people don't like shops to open on Sundays?
●What does your family buy on the internet?

TESCO

Open
7am - 10pm
& Sunday
10am - 4pm

café

cash

bakery

delicatessen

recycling

WHERE YOU LIVE
Do a survey of when and where your family goes shopping. You could make a chart with three columns, for 'When', 'Where' and 'What' you went to buy or look at.

Some things to think about

Here are some interesting things to think about when you go shopping. Were the goods made or grown in another country? What can you find out about that country? Many of the vegetables in this shop were grown in Kenya.

- Can you find Kenya on a globe or in an atlas?
- How is food transported from other countries to the UK?
- Which countries were your clothes made in?
- Can you find some 'Fairtrade' goods in your supermarket?

FRUIT PASSION™
FAIRTRADE JUICE
FAIRTRADE
Pure Tropical Juice
partially made from concentrate

Some goods from other countries are marked 'Fairtrade'. This means that people received fair pay for growing or making these goods.

Can you recycle the bags, boxes and other containers in which your shopping is wrapped?

- Why do shops give bags with their name on?
- Why is it bad to throw away plastic in the rubbish that goes to landfill sites?
- How much money does the shop want people to spend on teddy bears (below)?
- What would you do if you only wanted one teddy bear?

WHERE YOU LIVE
Talk about what you can do to recycle more and throw away less.

Get your paws on us this Christmas

3 FOR 2 or £5 each

AN EXTRA 10% OFF

EVERYTHING IN STORE when you spend £5 or more

HURRY! Today Only

Shopkeepers want you to buy things, so that they can make more money. Do you think that special offers might make people spend more than they wanted to spend?

Glossary

Arcade A narrow, covered passageway with shops on either side.

Assistants Helpers.

Banks Organisations that keep people's money for them, and help to pass money from one person to another.

Brochures Leaflets or booklets that publicise things.

Building societies Organizations that, like banks, keep people's money for them.

Chains Groups of shops in different places owned by the same company, which have the same name and sell the same goods.

Charity shops Shops that sell goods to raise money for a particular charity. Many of the goods are second-hand.

Checkouts Desks where people go to pay at a supermarket or other large, self-service shop.

Companies Business organisations that aim to make money. Many large companies have branches all over the world.

Counter A table where goods are shown or money is counted.

Customers People who may buy things from a shop, or who use the service that is offered at a shop or other place.

Department store A large shop made up of many different departments, often on several floors. Each department sells a different type of goods.

Estate agents Shops that buy, sell and rent houses and flats for people.

Goods Things that are bought and sold.

Groceries Foods and household things, such as washing-up liquid.

Hospice A place to stay for people who are very ill indeed.

Logo A company's symbol.

Mall A shopping centre, all under one roof.

Newsagents Shops that sell newspapers.

Parade A row of shop buildings.

Retail park A group of shops around a large car parking area. Many retail parks are near a main road, on the edge of a town.

Second-hand Already used by someone else.

Self-service Where customers take the goods they want from the shop shelves themselves and then pay for them at a checkout.

Shopping precinct An area of shops around a space that is usually for pedestrians only.

Stalls Tables or stands, where things are displayed for sale.

Stationery All kinds of paper and writing materials.

Stock room The room behind a shop where goods are stored before they are displayed or sold.

Supermarket A large, self-service shop that sells food and household things.

Take-aways Shops that sell food ready to eat, such as sandwiches, pizzas and fish and chips.

Till The drawer where money is kept, at a shop's counter.

Traders People who buy and sell goods.

Travel agent A shop that provides information about travel, especially to foreign countries.

Volunteers People who work for no pay, because they want to help.

Further information

http://www.woodlands-junior.kent.sch.uk/customs/topics/index.htm has useful information for projects about Britain. You can look up a topic, such as Shops, in the long A to Z list.

You can find out what a shop was like 100 years ago at http://www.j-sainsbury.co.uk/museum/youngvm.htm

At the Castle Museum in York you can walk about in reconstructions of streets, with shops from Victorian and Edwardian times. http://www.york.castle.museum/

Beamish: North of England Open Air Museum is a living, working experience of life as it was in the North in the early 1800s and 1900s. It includes a recreation of a street from a market town in 1913. http://www.beamish.org.uk/

Books

A Walk in the Town, Sally Hewitt, 2005 (Franklin Watts)

I Can Help Recycle Rubbish, Viv Smith, 2001 (Franklin Watts)

Just the Job: I Work in a Supermarket, Clare Oliver, 2004 (Franklin Watts)

Look Around You: In a City, Ruth Thomson, 2007 (Wayland)

Making a Difference: Reducing Rubbish, Sue Barraclough, 2006 (Franklin Watts)

Our Local Area: Shops, Jeff Stanfield, 2006 (Wayland)

Why Manners Matter: Going Shopping, Jillian Powell, 2005 (Franklin Watts)

Index

30